Inspirational Rhymes

Inspirational Rhymes

Recycled Souls

Chavanese Wint

Published by Icons Media Publishing in 2024

Copyright © Chavanese Wint

First Edition

The author asserts the moral right under the Copyright, Designs and Patents Act 1988 to be identified as the author of this work.

All Rights reserved. No part of this publication may be reproduced, stored in a retrieval system or transmitted, in any form or by any means without the prior consent of the author, nor be otherwise circulated in any form of binding or cover other than that in which it is published and without a similar condition being imposed on the subsequent purchaser.

CONTENTS

Faith *1*

Being Selective *2*

The Reason *3*

Many Are Called *5*

You Are What You Eat *6*

Like You Can *8*

Sinning *10*

Life is What you Make it *12*

Missing you *13*

Time *14*

The Silent Weeper *16*

Punches *18*

Age of Innocence *20*

The Pain *22*

The Perfectionist *24*

Words Don't Faze Me *25*

His Money *26*

The Pain of Missing You *28*

Unequal Society *29*

Let's Rhyme *30*

Invisibility............32

My Thinking 33

Lost............34

Pull Through 36

My Human Body............38

Opinions 40

The Wind 41

Faithless 42

Car Crash............44

Death............45

Manipulation............47

Cheat & Deceit............48

God's Creatures............49

If No One Marries Me 50

Deep Within............51

It's Time............52

An Opened Mouth............53

Risk............55

Owners Gain 57

Beauty of Your Reflection............58

I Love You! 59

Alive 61

The Wrong Pearls *63*
Giving Up *64*
Released *65*
Pins and Needles *67*
Who's Wrong? *68*
Reconsider *69*
The Mourner *71*
The Better You Get *72*

DEDICATION

Then, with this newfound understanding, it became clear to me that we are not just mere beings existing on this planet, but rather recycled souls that have traversed the vast expanse of the universe. We are all interconnected, intertwined in a cosmic dance that spans galaxies. Each soul carries within it a unique history, shaped by countless lifetimes and experiences. Our existence is not limited to this earthly realm; instead, we are part of a grand tapestry woven by the cosmos. It is through this realization that we can truly appreciate the beauty and significance of our collective journey through space and time. As we gaze up at the stars, let us remember that we are not alone - we are surrounded by the echoes of our past lives and the potential for infinite futures.

To: Shermaine Campbell

Faith

Time: 22:12
Date: 7.10.14

Faith, it comes when you least expect it,
Never to be **corrected**,
It's **connected** to our **soul** and **mind**,
Infected with the ability to have hope; but with freedom in mind.

~

Faith, it's never to be **subjected**,
But respected as a human in time,
To live without *fear* but to have peace of mind.

~

Faith, it's the strength that carries **peace** within our **souls**,
To have faith deep within, you cannot have room for holes.

~

Faith, is when you think about your **goals**,
You think about your life, then you take control.

~

Faith, it's the **gift** that keeps on **shining**,
It's the one that tells you, never you stop smiling.

~

When you have **faith**, there is no room for **whining**,
If you want to become the next best-seller, then never stop **signing**.

~

Faith. X

Being Selective

Time: 3:47
Date: 2.12.14

Just because you close your eyes,
it doesn't mean you're at rest,
Life's journey is filled with struggles and hardship,
putting you to the test.

~

You've poured your heart into your career,
Your family, and all that you hold dear,
But finding peace and commitment is what you need to persevere.

~

Time slips through our fingers like sand, we have no control,
Yet it's in these moments of uncertainty,
That our true strength unfolds.

~

Stop playing the victim, don't let life dictate your fate,
Embrace your talents and blessings,
let go of the pursuit for wealth and wait.

~

For true fulfilment lies not in material possessions or success alone, but in living a life of purpose, making an impact that will be known.

So rise above the challenges, embrace each moment with zest, and remember, just because you sleep, it doesn't mean you're truly at rest.

The Reason

Time: 04:14
Date: 2.12.14

Everything happens for a reason,
All the years and the months, even the minutes is a season.
STOP! Look at life with a new perspective,
Instead of chasing money and power, let's be more reflective.

~

In the cold, you stood there freezing,
Feeling the pain deepen within, it was appeasing.
At the bus stop, you encountered Steven,
His asymmetrical features left you wondering'.

~

As time goes on, your body may weaken,
A big cold may come, leaving you sneezing'.
And in those moments of vulnerability,
Beware of negativity's ability.

~

But remember, everything happens for a reason,
Each experience shaping us throughout each season.
So embrace life's challenges and lessons taught,
For in these trials, our true strength is sought.

~

It's time for a fresh start, a new chapter to begin,
Release the weight of past regrets and let your spirit win,
Believe in yourself and the power within your soul,
And watch as your dreams unfold, making you whole.

~

Your degree is almost within reach, just a few steps away,
Open the doors to success and let your talents sway,

The world is waiting for your brilliance to shine,
So keep pushing forward and never decline.

~

In the hills, among the stars, is where you'll truly belong,
Where melodies of success will become your song.
Embrace this journey, soar high above the sky,
And remember, no dream is too far or too high.

Many Are Called

2008

Many are called, but only few are **chosen**,
We are living in a **society,** where many hearts gets **broken**.

~

One **bullet** to the head, three stabs to the **womb,**
Mummy starts crying, but she doesn't know it's <u>WHO</u>.

~

One step **forward**, two steps **back.**
Why do we remain the same?
Well, only God knows that.

~

Take it or **leave** it, but he's coming very **soon**,
One day we will be at **peace**,
You will find out very **soon**.

You Are What You Eat

Time: 3:39
Date: 18/2/15

They say that you are what you eat,
So does that mean that I am a vegetable, or I am a meat?
WAIT! So am I a grain of wheat?
Because I consume nourishing foods that keep me upbeat.
This notion of identity through diet is quite discrete.

~

Wait, let me repeat.
Am I a spoonful of ice cream in the summer heat?
Indulging in sweet treats, feeling oh so elite,
But there's more to me than just what I eat.

~

I am a canvas, ready to create,
An artist with words, painting stories with every slate.
I am a dreamer, reaching for the stars and never late,
Fueling my aspirations with passion and faith.

~

I am a warrior, fighting battles both big and small,
Overcoming obstacles, standing tall.
I am a beacon of positivity, spreading light to all,
Inspiring others to rise and answer the call.

~

So while food plays its part in shaping who we may be,
There's more to our essence than what we see.
We are complex beings, filled with vitality,
Connected by love and humanity.

~

Oh look, a piece of crab meat.
Now don't worry, you know that I am really quite petite,

I'll think about the consequences when I go on my retreat.
Hmm MEAT! But let's not forget, there's more to life than just what we eat.

It's about finding joy and following our heart's beat.
So let's embrace the moments, both big and small,
And let inspiration guide us through it all.
For in every challenge lies an opportunity,
To grow, to learn, and set our spirits free.
So let's seize the day and make each moment count,
With courage and determination, we will surmount.

Like You Can

Time: 11:47
Date: 7.19.14

You can be a dreamer, chasing stars in the night,
You can be a writer, penning stories that ignite,
You can be an artist, painting colors so bright,
For no one can live it like YOU can.

~

You can be a traveler, exploring lands afar,
You can be a teacher, shaping minds like a shining star,
You can be a scientist, unraveling mysteries so bizarre,
But remember, no one can live it like YOU can.

~

You can be a leader, inspiring others to soar,
You can be a caregiver, giving love and more,
You can be a mentor, guiding those who implore,
Because only you can live life like YOU can.

~

So embrace your uniqueness, let your light shine through,
The world needs your voice and all that you do,
With each step you take and every path you pursue,
Remember, no one can live it like YOU.

~

Embrace your passions, unleash your art,
Let your creativity ignite and impart.
For within you lies a spark so bright,
That can illuminate even the darkest night.

~

Believe in yourself, trust in your voice,
Break free from the chains and make your choice.

You have the power to shape your destiny,
And create a life that's truly extraordinary.
~

So don't let anyone tell you who you should be,
Because only YOU can define your own journey.

Sinning

Time: 23:10
Date: 4.19.14

After morning, oh crap, this is a mess,
All the makeup is now gone, even my pretty little dress.
But I won't stress, for I know beauty lies within,
A confident smile and a heart that's genuine.

~

Yes, my appearance may have faded away,
But my inner strength will never sway.
I'll embrace the imperfections that I possess,
For they make me unique and truly blessed.

~

No need for tissue or fake enhancements,
I'll embrace my natural self with no pretence.
For true beauty shines from deep within,
It's not about the outside, but the person within.

~

So let go of societal standards and expectations,
Embrace your flaws and rise above limitations.

~

One wrong move, then you can forget all the rest,
Just believe and always remember that life is a test.
Life will let you go then show you the way to success.
Yes, no more partying and feeling all depressed,
Because life is a dream and you will never be suppressed.

~

Embrace the challenges that come your way,
For they are opportunities in disguise, leading to a brighter day.

~

Remember, one misstep does not define your fate,
It's how you rise from it that truly resonates.
Believe in yourself and let go of doubt,
For the power within you is what life is all about.

Life Is What You Make It

2007

Life is what you make it, a canvas to paint,
With colours of joy, love, and strength, no restraint.
Embrace the power within, let your dreams ignite,
For in this journey called life, you hold the spotlight.

~

Whether you choose it or not, life's path unfolds,
Opportunities and challenges, stories yet untold.
Take pride in what you do, with every step you take,
And watch as your efforts and passions awake.

~

Have confidence and dignity in yourself each day,
Believe in your worth and let self-doubt fade away.
Then make life as you should, with purpose and grace,
Leaving behind a legacy that time can never erase.

~

I am thinking about life's endless possibilities,
The adventures that await, the triumphs and vulnerabilities.
I am thinking about carving my own destiny,
Embracing every moment with gratitude and serenity.

~

I am thinking about the lessons learned along the way,
The resilience gained from hardships faced each day.
I am thinking about growth, both inside and out,
And how I can make a positive impact without a doubt.

Missing You

2007

Trying to rest my head on the **soft rectangular white fluffy pillow**,

~

But at the same time with *tears* running down my face,
Like a **cloud** getting ready to burst with **rain**.

~

Drip by drip,
One by one,
Tears slowly running down my **face**,
Memories after **memories.**

~

<u>His face in my head, like a stone cold picture.</u>
When he laughs his face **connects** to my **heart**,
His hugs also connecting to my **body**.

~

It's astonishing how I am **emotionally** stunned by him.
Now the only thing that is going through my head is these **words**.

~

From *comma* to full **STOP**!
Every **abbreviation** connected to my <u>mind,</u>
My mind and my body, lost in time.

~

I'll wait forever if I have too, I thought to **myself**....

Time

Time: 18:21
Date: 28.9.2014

Time does heal, but it heals very slowly,
In the depths of darkness, I felt so lonely.
My body and my mind, consumed by despair,
Longing for someone to show that they care.

~

Help me find the strength to carry this weight,
To rise above the struggles and not hesitate.
With your guidance and support, I'll be strong,
And together we'll prove that we belong.

~

Let's turn this pain into a story of resilience,
A tale of overcoming every obstacle with brilliance.
I'll harness my talents and chase my dreams,
No longer held back by doubt or self-esteem.

~

Each day, I'll rise with determination in my eyes,
No more dwelling on failures or past goodbyes.
With your inspiration, my spirit will soar,
And I'll conquer life's challenges like never before.

~

I was one step closer, maybe even more,
But, day-by-day I just couldn't find a cure.
Backtracked into the past, couldn't handle it anymore,
My heart was broken, it felt so sore.

~

Now you're gone, I've accepted that you won't come back,
But one thing is for sure; you knew how to act.
I miss your little face when it was looking so whack,
But we will meet again soon, no matter where you're at.

~

In the depths of despair, I sought solace and light,
Seeking answers to ease my pain and make things right.

Through trials and tribulations, I learned to endure,
Finding strength within myself, becoming more pure.

~

Though the road may be long and filled with strife,
I refuse to give up on this beautiful life.
With every setback and failure that comes my way,
I'll rise above and conquer, come what may.

~

So here's to moving forward, leaving the past behind,
Embracing the present with an open mind.
For even in darkness, there's always a glimmer of hope,
A chance for redemption and a new way to cope.

The Silent Weeper

2007

I call myself the silent weeper,
That person who only cries in the dark.
That person who locks themselves away from everything and everyone,
That person, who cannot talk.

~

But within these tears, lies a strength untold,
A resilience that cannot be easily broken or sold.
For every night spent in fear and doubt,
I rise each day with a flame burning within, ready to shout.

~

I refuse to be defined by the words they say,
Or let their cruelty darken my way.
For I am more than the pain they inflict,
I am a warrior, determined to uplift.

~

No longer will I allow their taunts to define my worth,
I will shine like a diamond, despite my place of birth.
With every tear shed in secret despair, I find solace in knowing there's courage hidden there.

~

Or you can try this one,
Maybe if I write a poem, my pain will be undone.
Maybe, just maybe if I find solace in rhyme,
I can heal my wounds and find peace in time.

~

It's not the darkness that defines me, but the light within,
So let me rise above the shadows and let my spirit sing.
For in this journey of life, I refuse to surrender,
I'll embrace the challenges and become stronger,
not tender.

~

So don't judge me by my silent tears,
For within them lies strength beyond years.
I may be that person you overlook and ignore,
But deep within me, an unbreakable spirit does soar.

Punches

Time: 02:11
Date: 28.11.14

I don't like to throw punches,
No kicks or crunches, I like to maybe choke,
Hold it down, face up, no sponges.

~

I prefer to rise above the hate,
To spread love and not berate,
With words that inspire and elevate,
In a world that can sometimes frustrate.

~

I believe in the power of kindness,
To heal wounds and erase blindness,
A simple act can bring lightness,
And turn darkness into brightness.

~

So let us be the change we seek,
To uplift others when they feel weak,
With compassion, empathy, and a cheeky sneak,
Of laughter to make their spirits peak.

~

Together we can build a world so grand,
Where unity and understanding expand,
Hand in hand, we'll make a stand,
For love and peace across the land.

~

The devil's deceit knows no bounds,
His lies echoing through the air.
With no regard for honor or respect,
He thrives on holding grudges unfair.
But I won't let his words break me down,
For I am stronger than I seem.
Like a resilient flower in a storm,
I'll rise above and fulfill my dream.

Age Of Innocence

Time: 4:26am
Date: 29.10.2014

I was so small and innocent,
I grew up in a place where I could only be an immigrant.
Coming from a land where opportunities were limited,
To a country where dreams were vivid.

~

With determination and strength, I faced each day,
Knowing that success was just a step away.
I refused to let ignorance define my worth,
And set out to prove my value on this earth.

~

Though the journey was tough, I never lost sight,
Of the goals I had set and the dreams shining bright.
I fought against adversity with all my might,
And embraced the challenges, both day and night.

~

My team is a militant, they've got Intelligence,
Not even half of your army could ever have relevance.
With minds sharp and thoughts profound,
We conquer challenges and turn them around.

~

In this world where innocence seems to fade,
We seek salvation through the paths we've laid.
Exploring desires, embracing our curiosity,
Yet cautious of the consequences, we strive for clarity.

~

Life's choices can be tough to bear,
But perseverance will lead us to a future fair.
Praying with grace and humble demeanour,
We manifest dreams, creating a life much cleaner.

The Pain

Time: 18:48pm
Date: 28.8.2014

One hour has passed since we spoke,
My heart heavy with worry and hope.
Where are you at, my friend?
Are you facing demons or finding a new path to mend?
My chest feels tight, as if it might crack,
But I won't let despair take me back.
Those sweet messages we shared now seem distant and cold, But I hold onto the memories like stories yet untold.

~

As the morning sun rises, I wake with a lump in my throat,
A sense of unease that refuses to float.
I reach for my phone, hoping for a sign,
but silence greets me like an unwelcome shrine.
Anger boils within me, ready to ignite,
As I wonder if you realize the pain of your flight.
But amidst the frustration and anger's glow,
I still hold onto hope that someday you'll show.

~

So wherever you are, my dear friend,
Know that in this journey, my support will never end.
I'll wait for your return with open arms and a forgiving heart, And together we'll mend what once fell apart.

~

I am angry as hell now, I hope you bloody know,
But through my anger,
A glimmer of understanding began to show.

For though I don't believe in spirits, I felt your presence near, A comforting touch, a whispered voice,
Wiping away my tears.
My sweet baby boy has gone, dear God please hear me,
But in this moment of grief, I know you are with me.

~

How could this happen?
The question echoes in my mind,
Yet deep within my heart, a sense of peace I find.
For even though the pain is unbearable, the loss so profound, I know that love transcends all boundaries, forever unbound. One hour ago, you said sweetie, I love you dearly,
And now in this darkness, your love shines so clearly.

~

This is not a dream; it's a reality I must face,
But with your memory as my guiding light, I'll find grace.
No longer will worry consume me like a cup overflowing,
Instead, I'll embrace each moment with gratitude growing.
Though my soul feels heavy and on the verge of dropping,
I know that your spirit lives on, forever never stopping.

The Perfectionist

Time: 12:24am
Date: 20.2.15

I aspire to be a perfectionist,
Strumming the guitar like an instrumentalist.

~

Yearning to be flawless, never missing a beat,
Singing the highest notes, my voice pure and sweet.

~

In all tasks, I aim for perfection,
Assisting others with meticulous attention.

~

No corner uncleaned, no task left undone,
I'll be your perfect helper, never outdone.

~

If you desire more affection in our connection,
I'll shower you with kisses, like a love specialist.

~

An artist of expression, that's what I long to be,
Spreading love and optimism for all to see.

~

So if you seek a partner who aims for the best,
Be ready to award me the medallist's crest.

Words Don't Faze Me

2009

Words don't **faze** me,
And neither do YOU!

~

Your *lips* are **lying**,
But your **actions** are telling the **truth.**

~

Your *ears* may **hear**,
But my *eyes* can **see**,
Now what are those *words* really **telling** me?

~

You're **lying** about *something* and you'll soon **regret** it,
Your *words* don't **faze** me, so just **forget** it.

His Money

Time: 3:06am
Date: 18.2.15

He said he's the king and he makes all the money,
As he puts his feet up, his ego starts to rise and be sunny.
But honey, don't let his words make you feel small,
You're strong and capable, standing tall.

~

He may claim to hold all the power,
But remember, you have your own tower.
You don't need validation from a man like him,
Your worth is not determined by his whims.

~

So go ahead, chase your dreams with pride,
Don't let his arrogance push you aside.
You are more than just a servant or a wife,
You have the strength to create your own life.

~

"Am I a dummy," you ask?
No, my dear, I am much more than that.
I am your husband,
The one who stands by your side through thick and thin.
But please, my love, can you cook me a curry?
For I am a rich man, not a poor man who is down in the gully.

~

Oh darling child, go and tell your mother with care,
For her jokes may not be the best to share.

If she keeps up this behavior,
There will be no Easter bunny to bring joy and delight.
Let us strive to keep our spirits bright.

~

Now my sweet, I am famished and yearning for a treat.
Go ahead and whip up something delicious to eat.
I'll be waiting patiently in my chair,
Counting out my lovely money with flair.
Oh, the taste of that curry will surely be beyond compare.

~

So let's savor each bite and indulge in this feast divine.
For together we'll create moments that forever shine.
And as we dine with laughter and glee,
We'll embrace the richness of life that sets us free.

The Pain of Missing You

Time: 19:09
Date: 28.9.2014

They took you from me and I don't know why,
On the first day I met you, you said, girl, you are so shy.
You broke all the bridges, yes you broke every wall,
But now you're gone, I don't believe I'll be standing very tall.

~

Our late conversations were always just the best,
All those fights, all those little things,
YES, you made a bloody mess.
My bones are weak and my heart is now broken,
But I will NEVER let you go; I will keep you as my token.

~

Relied on prescriptions to keep my head uptight,
I couldn't sleep, I couldn't eat, it didn't feel right.
But how could this happen? How did we drift apart?
From love's sweet melody to a shattered heart.

~

I'll pick up the pieces and find strength in the pain,
For I know deep within, there's sunshine after the rain.
I'll rise above this darkness and learn to let go,
Because life goes on, even when love says no.

Unequal Society

2009

We are living in an unequal society,
Everywhere we go there's no morality.
No shame, just grief, And a whole lot of stress,
There's no wonder our lives is in a whole load of mess.

~

But amidst the chaos and despair,
We must rise above and show we care.
In this world of inequality and strife,
Let's be the ones to bring back life.

~

With empathy and kindness in our hearts,
Let's rebuild what has been torn apart.
No matter our differences or where we're from,
Together, we can create a world that's fair for everyone.

~

So let's stop pushing and shaming one another,
And instead support each other like sisters and brothers.
For only when we stand united as a team,
Can we turn this nightmare into a beautiful dream.

Let's Rhyme

Time: 05:59am
Date: 29.10.2014

He said manipulate, I said dedicate,
He said, baby don't you dare try interrogate.
I said liberate, he says I'll penetrate,
I said, do what you're doing but don't manipulate.

~

"Girl don't you hesitate," "But boy, I wasn't on a date",
"Girl I saw you partying in the club, talking about celebrate."

~

Now let me demonstrate, Oh boy, I need to go premeditate,
Hell no, no you don't, don't let me go and relocate.

~

I ain't even gonna investigate, Got no time to educate,
Just gonna turn my back and walk away and maybe desolate.

~

In this world of manipulation and lies,
I choose dedication and truth as my prize.
No need to interrogate or question your ways,
I'll liberate myself from your deceitful plays.

~

You say you'll penetrate my heart and mind,
But I won't let your toxic presence bind.

I'll do what I must with love and grace,
And free myself from this suffocating space.

~

Yes, I'll be devastated if we're torn apart,
But I won't speculate on what went wrong from the start,
I'll just believe what you say, trust in your heart,
And try not to perpetuate any feelings of doubt or depart.

~

Our love is worth fighting for, it's not a debate,
Let's hold on tight and navigate through any storms we may face,
Together we can conquer anything, no matter the weight,
And learn to relegate the challenges that come our way with grace.

~

So let's inseminate our love with hope and resilience,
Never taking each other for granted,
Always showing persistence,
In this journey of love, let's embrace every instance,
And build a future together filled with joy and brilliance.

~

So don't hesitate to be true to yourself,
Don't let others dictate your worth or health.
Celebrate who you are and all that you bring,
And let your liberation be the song that you sing.

Invisibility

2008

Nothing can kill me because I am already dead,
It's like I'm a ghost with skin, an invisible thread.
You can look at me, but not truly see,
Touch me, yet fail to feel the real me.

~

You listen to my words, but don't hear the pain,
Dance with me, but your steps remain the same.
Kiss me, but your love feels untrue,
Love me, but not being in love with you.

~

You care for me, yet never about my soul,
Trust in me, but never make me whole.
You're there when you're with me, yet deny my presence,
Leaving me haunted by this cruel essence.

My Thinking

Time: 12:26am
Date: 29.3.2012

I am just like the wind, all I want to do is pass through,
I just want a little more time, to do what I do.

~

I think like the waves,
But, I move like the sea,
My brain is contagious, I'm addicted to me.

~

even though I think like the waves, but my purpose is clear,
To inspire and uplift, spreading positivity far and near.
With each breath, I carry hope and dreams,
Whispering encouragement in gentle streams.

~

I am a force of nature, unstoppable and free,
Guiding others towards their destiny.
In my presence, doubts are blown away,
Leaving room for courage to pave the way.

~

I am the voice that echoes in your soul,
Reminding you that you are whole.
Embrace the power within your core,
And let your spirit soar forevermore.

Lost

2007

It's like I am **tucked** up into a small shell,
Not to be **seen** or **heard.**
Just separated from **everything** and **everyone**,
Not **seeing** the world for what it's really like.

~

It's like I am this **small** person in this **big** and *cruel* world,
Just waiting to **exhale**….
Just waiting for someone to come and **rescue** me,
And to take me out of this **unforgettable** life that I am living.

~

My **thoughts** and dreams **shattered**,
Never, to be **seen** or **heard.**
Just **locked** up in a small box, with the key being thrown away.

I wonder to myself, as I write in my note-book.

~

Will it be like this **forever?**
Lonely and **cold**,
Feeling as if you are the only person in this world,
Feeling **trapped** and **unsafe.**

Despite my *fears* to the world, All I can do is **wait.**

~

Wait until someone finally realises that I **exists**,

And to see that I am a **human** being just like them,
And all I want is for someone to love me,
And to show me the **real** reason why I am on this ***EARTH***

Pull Through

Time: 3:18am
Date: 20.2.15

You need to pull yourself together, my friend,
For the journey ahead, you must transcend.
Though the road may be tough and steep,
In your heart, determination runs deep.

~

You have to pull through, no matter the cost,
Even when all hope seems to be lost.
Do you think that anyone out there can face the challenges
with as much flair?

~

You're a shining light in a world so dark,
With every step, leaving your mark.
Embrace the strength within your soul,
And watch as your dreams begin to unfold.

~

Believe in yourself and never give in,
Success is waiting for you to begin.
Keep pushing forward, don't look back,
There's no limit to what you can attract.

~

So gather your courage and stand tall,
Together we'll conquer any wall.
The power lies within your hands,
To shape your destiny and reach new lands.

~

Pull yourself together, my dear friend,
For this journey is not yet at its end.
Through every trial and tribulation,
You'll emerge with newfound inspiration.

My Human Body

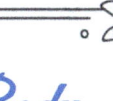

Time: 08:59pm
Date: 1.12.2009

My **mind** is like the **sea,**
And my **brain** is like the **sand**,
It doesn't **listen**,
It just **understands**.

~

My **human** body is like the **train,**
It only **rolls** on a **track**,
It never **rolls** off,
I hope you'll be ok with that.

~

My **soul** is like **ice** and my **heart** burns **fire**.
Choose one to stick to, it's your **desire**.

~

My **eyes** see **clearly,** it doesn't need a **check,**
So think very carefully, before you write that **cheque.**
My **thoughts** are like a **plane**, it's hard to **slow** down,
Only when I am **ready**, to jump out and hit the ground.
My mind is like the sea, and my brain is like the sand,
It doesn't listen, It just understands.

~

My spirit soars high, like a bird in the sky,
Unfettered and free, never asking why.
With every breath I take, I feel alive,
Embracing each moment, ready to thrive.

~

My words flow like a river, gentle and calm,
Carrying messages of hope and charm.
I weave them together, creating a tapestry,
Inspiring others with my poetic alchemy.

~

In the depths of my being, creativity resides,
A spark that ignites, where passion abides.
I paint with words, a canvas of dreams,
Guiding souls towards infinite streams.

~

So let my voice echo through the ages,
Spreading love, wisdom, in courageous pages.
For in this vast universe, I stand tall and true,
A vessel of inspiration, forever anew.

Opinions

Time: 3:41am
Date: 19.2.15

People's opinion is one thing that I hate,
Especially when they try to dictate who I can or cannot date. They may not be my parents,
But they seem to think they have the authority to control my fate.

~

Let's engage in a debate and set things straight.
However, their hatred only fuels our laughter,
As we enjoy our blissful life upstate,
Surrounded by the abundance of our luxurious estates.

~

Instead of wasting time hating on us,
Why don't they focus on creating their own illusions of desperate companions?

~

After all, it is not their approval that we seek; rather, it is God's blessing that guides us as we walk through the gates of His divine love and grace. So let them continue to voice their judgments while we cherish the freedom to love and live according to our own desires.

The Wind

2007

I lay there **quietly**, but **gently**,
Listening to the rain **beat** against my <u>window</u>.

~

The **wind** begins to move **sharply** into my <u>room</u>.

Reminding me why it's there
By knocking off all the light bottles on my **dressing table**.

~

It then starts to move *slowly,* but **gently**,
Taking <u>control</u> of me.

At the *same* time,
Putting all the ***<u>broken</u>*** pieces of my **body** back **together**.

~

It *continues* on by taking away all my **pain** and **frustration**.
At the same time, covering me with its ***cool*** and **unforgettable** *presence*.

Faithless

Time: 21:56pm
Date: 3.12.14

So I heard you say, you are faithless.
But you ain't dateless,
You're only giving up on hope and acting ageless.

~

But you're just aimless,
Talking about weightless,
Yet every time I see you in McDonald's, you're acting shameless.

~

In my opinion you're just careless,
It has nothing to do with you being faithless,
Faith has a meaning, definition, YES! It is fearless.

~

So now it's all about awareness, you have to be tearless,
Harden your heart and fight those battles with fierceness.

~

Open your eyes and see the evil at its clearest,
So that you, can never be tamed and act cheerless.

~

But remember, faith is not just an empty concept,
It's a conviction that keeps us intact.

~

Don't let doubts make your spirit retract,
Embrace the unknown with an unwavering pact.

~

Believe in yourself, don't accept defeat as fact,
For faith gives us strength to overcome any act.

~

It's not about being naive or blind,
But trusting in something greater, aligned.

~

Have faith in the journey that lies ahead,
And let fear and uncertainty be shed.

~

So don't give up on hope or feel forsaken,
With faith by your side, you'll never be shaken.

Car Crash

Time: 09:50pm
Date: 1.12.2009

Slow down, my friend, don't let time slip away,
Why rush through life when you can savor each day?

~

In the chaos of speed, we often lose control,
Leaving us broken and searching for a way to console.

~

Take a breath, find solace in stillness and peace,
For it is in moments of calm that our souls find release.

~

The pain may be spreading like wildfire inside,
But with patience and healing, we can begin to reside.

~

Amidst the wreckage and the crimson-stained floor,
We face the consequences of a collision we didn't ask for.

~

Let's remember that accidents happen, mistakes are made,
It's how we learn and grow from them that will never fade.

Death

2007

There she is, just **laying** there,
All on her **own**.

~

It's been **four** months now since she's gone,
Sometimes I wonder if anyone **remembers,** or even **thinks** about her.

~

I believe that if **God** isn't *ready* for someone,
Then you should never take that person's ***life.***

~

I never even knew her,
But I wonder if anyone feels the **guilt** and **sadness** that I felt for Her.

~

She's just down there in that **coffin,**
Her **flesh** turning to **bones**,
And her **bones** turning to **ashes**.

Little **animals** *crawling* all over her,
She can't ***breathe*** or **move**.
Her eyes closed **gently**, as she disappears into the **hands** of the Lord.

~

Just **drifting** off,
Forgetting about the world and everything in it.
Meeting **family, friends** and maybe even **enemies**.

She was so young some people might say,
She had her whole life ahead of her.

~

But now she's **gone** and there is **nothing** that anyone can say
Or do, to bring her back.

Manipulation

Time: 2:25am
Date: 18.2.15

Manipulation stems from deep-rooted fears,
A facade of falsehood, shedding crocodile tears.
But I won't be swayed by your deceitful play,
I see through your act, I won't go astray.

~

If only you had shown a hint of empathy,
Our connection could have blossomed beautifully.
Yet your behavior remains a constant distraction,
I refuse to be ensnared in your web of dissatisfaction.

~

You anticipate your own actions,
Then try to discriminate my reaction,
Then when I intimidate your attraction,
You turn things into your own satisfaction.

~

It's time to be authentic, to show who you are,
Transform your manipulation into actions that leave no scar. Perhaps then, just maybe, I'll start to feel contractions,
A glimmer of hope amidst all the distractions.

~

Only time will reveal the truth in its entirety,
Maybe what I truly need is your absence entirely.
But we will never know until we let go and grow,
In this journey of self-discovery, only time will show.

Cheat & Deceit

Time: 2:40am
Date: 20.2.15

Cheat and deceit, a dangerous duo that should never meet,
Their intentions are dark, filled with deceit.
They lure you in with promises of treats,
But behind their smiles, they plan your defeat.

~

Their words are like quicksand, never concrete,
They'll claim innocence while leaving you incomplete.
Be cautious of their sweet gestures so discreet,
For they will turn on you and leave you in the street.

~

Stand tall and strong, don't let them mistreat,
Expose their lies and never accept defeat.
With honesty and integrity, take a seat,
And watch as their web of deceit is unthreaded, neat.

God's Creatures

2007

The **birds** are ***singing,*** as I lay there quietly in my bed,
I can hear them *through* my **open** *window.*

~

Their *song sounding* very **unrehearsed**,
But yet, it has an **unstoppable** great *rhythm*.

At this point I am very **relaxed**,
feeling very **honored,** to know that **God** can **create** such
Beautiful *creatures,*
With such **wonderful** powers.

~

To get *deep* within your **soul**,
Deep within your **minds.**

Making you just want to grab **hold** of everything,
And **treasure** it, until the end of time.

If No One Marries Me

Time: 11:29pm
Date: 19.2.15

―― ᴆ ᴄ ᴆ ᴄ ――

If I grow up and no one marries me,
I shall have babies and be wild and free.
Because that's the key, to a brand-new me,
I was a lonely little girl, broken down in the sea.

~

But you don't agree?
You're telling me that I should go to church, and praise thee? But back when I was in the cells, no one came to visit me,
So leave me be. I shall be counting now from 1,2,3,
Just waiting… on my husband, to fall out of a tree.

~

It's up to me, and yes, I just want to be wild and free,
Just a pretty little girl, waiting on a man to marry me.
But as time goes by, I realize it's not about being tied down,
It's about embracing my independence and owning my crown.

Deep Within

Time: 08:36pm
Date: 16.6.2011

Just because I rock, that doesn't mean I am made of stones. But there is something in my heart that is worth so much more than gold. It doesn't matter about love, it doesn't matter about pain. The only thing I am worried about is that you don't see me in vain. I am going to make this a short one, but only for you to understand. I just want to let you know that my future is no longer in your hands. I was a woman of abuse, and I felt pain too. There are no words that could describe the pain I really felt inside. Now you can act like you know, but I can't make you understand. This is my life, filled with strife and yet full of hope and light.

It's Time

Time: 01:20pm
Date: 16.4.2011

The lights have struck, illuminating the stage,
As the audience gathers, eager to engage.
The dreams have faded, but a new chapter begins,
No more shadows lurking, no more hidden sins.

~

Tears have been shed, in moments of sorrow,
But through it all, you'll find a brighter tomorrow.
The darkness has lifted, leaving behind the pain,
Now it's time to rise and break free from the chain.

~

In times of grief, stress, and overwhelming hate,
Patience is tested, as we anxiously await.
To be released from the shackles of negativity,
Embracing a life filled with positivity and creativity.

~

It's your life now, in your hands it lies,
Make wise choices and let your soul rise.
For even in trials and tribulations so tough,
Stay true to yourself, for that is enough.

~

Remember, the Lord will bless you on this journey,
No matter what challenges you face eternally.
It's through hardships that strength is revealed,
So keep faith alive and let love be your shield.

An Opened Mouth

Time: 2:29am
Date: 18.2.14

A deceitful friend, oh what a curse they bring,
Their actions, like venomous snakes, they sting.
They wear masks of friendship so cleverly,
But their true intentions are hidden, you see.

~

They claim to hold their conscience so clear,
Yet behind closed doors, they spread rumours and jeer.
They shed crocodile tears to appear sincere,
But their words and actions only inspire fear.

~

They act accepting, especially towards the queer,
But deep down, their prejudice is crystal clear.
They'll throw you in an auction, ready to be sold,
To the highest bidder, your worth will be bold.

~

These friends love to play the role of an inner,
Passing judgment behind your back with a sinister glimmer. With self-righteousness, they claim to be winners,
But in truth, they're nothing more than sinners.

~

But sometimes in life, you have to try to be a little bolder,
For when it comes to achieving greatness, you can't simply shoulder.

~

Never lower yourself, trying to shine like a glitter,
Because we all know, a loose tongue always needs a zipper.

~

Instead, stand tall and strong, let your voice be heard,
Embrace the power of respect, let it spread like a bird.

~

Respect others' opinions, even if they differ from your own,
For in diversity lies strength and seeds of growth sown.

~

Treat everyone with kindness and empathy in your heart,
And watch as respect becomes an integral part.

~

Remember, respect is not just earned but also freely given,
So let it flow through your actions and decisions.

~

In this world where negativity sometimes runs wild,
Let respect be the guiding light that reconciles.

Risk

2009

I am going to take the risk of loving you, I am going to take the risk of life, I am going to take the risk of this opportunity, Because I know that I need you in my life.

~

I am going to risk my faith, I am going to risk my home, I am going to risk my life,
But I am not willing to risk my soul.

~

I am willing to risk my kids, I am willing to risk my wife, I am willing to risk cars, I am willing to lose my life.

~

I am now ready, to give it all up.
No more drinking Champagne, out of silly little cups.
It's about time now, that I start to buckle up, I am getting close to aging, so I have to stop.

~

Life is full of choices, risks we must embrace.
For love and happiness, we must sometimes chase.
Though uncertainties may come, and fears may arise,
We'll hold onto our dreams and reach for the skies.

~

With every step forward, we'll face the unknown,
In pursuit of a future where our hearts are truly shown.
We'll let go of material possessions and what they bring,

For in the grand scheme of things, they don't mean anything.

~

Our souls are precious, our spirits strong and true,
We won't compromise our values just for me or you.
We'll take risks for our family, sacrificing all we own,
Because love and loyalty are seeds that must be sown.

~

As time marches on and we grow old and gray,
We'll cherish every moment, making the most of each day.
No longer consumed by shallow desires or fleeting fame,
We'll focus on what truly matters, leaving behind a lasting name.

Owners Gain

Time: 2:18am
Date: 20.2.15

Some people's failure may bring them pain,
But don't let it discourage you or make you go insane.
When you stumble and fall, don't be afraid to rise,
You must gather your strength and give it another try.

~

They may be furious, they may shed tears,
Some might even write complaints out of their fears.
But you are strong and resilient, with unwavering belief,
Hold your ground and maintain your inner peace.

~

Feel the anger within, let it ignite your fire,
But remember to restrain yourself and rise higher.
Cool down your temper, show them how you've evolved,
Prove that you can overcome any problem unresolved.

~

Don't conform to their ways, stand out from the crowd,
You're a winner, so stand proud.
In due time, God will bless you and guide your way, Just keep pushing forward and seize the day.

Beauty Of Your Reflection
2011

Beauty ain't a gift,
But it can shine from many directions,
It's not just about your looks,
But the essence of your connections.

~

You could be flawed,
Or you can radiate grace,
It's not solely about appearance,
But the kindness in your embrace.

~

Don't judge others based on their exterior,
And never diminish what they possess,
You might have your own treasures too,
But appreciate what you possess.

~

Trust and have faith in yourself,
And always remember to be true,
Embrace the beauty of your reflections,
Embody the beauty within YOU!

I Love You!
Time: 09:10pm
Date: 3.12.14

ˋ ᘮ ᘯ ˊ

I just want to express my heartfelt affection for all of you,
To let you know that my love is steadfast and true.

~

If no one has ever uttered these words to your ears,
Or if it's been a while since they've erased your fears,
Just know that I hold you dear in my heart,
And my love for you will never depart.

~

As the weeks, months and years pass by,
There may be moments when you feel like you can't fly,
But remember, through every stumble and fall,
I'll be there to catch you, standing tall.

~

If you've experienced the pain of losing someone close,
Believe that they're watching over you, like a heavenly host.
In their presence, find solace and joy,
Knowing they're smiling down on us, like a child with a favourite toy.

~

You're a soldier of passion, a warrior of rhyme,
Your words cut through barriers, transcending space and time.

~

With each verse you craft, you paint a vivid scene,
Transporting listeners to places they've never been.

~

Your rhymes are like weapons, sharp and precise,
Leaving your opponents in awe of your lyrical might.

~

But remember, dear poet, as you conquer new lands,
Stay true to yourself and the power in your hands.

~

For it's not just about winning battles or gaining fame,
It's about touching hearts and leaving an everlasting flame.

#

Time: 21:33
Date: 3.12.14

It's the fact that you are still living this life,
It's the fact that you are still breathing,
It's the fact that you are still able to open your eyes,
It's a fact that you are still existing.

~

Even though the struggles seems like they are not easing,
What you don't know is, that your life is on the verge of completing.

~

So no regrets and no more beatings,
God will start the healing,
But you need to get on your knees and start to look to the ceiling.

~

True love has a different feeling,
So please get to know the right meaning,
He will come along with all the flowers and the cheating.

~

In this journey of life, where shadows may appear,
Remember that rhymes can bring joy and cheer.
Embrace each moment with a hopeful heart,
For every ending, there's a brand new start.

~

Amidst the chaos and trials we face,

Believe in yourself and embrace grace.
The struggles may seem overwhelming at times,
But remember, life is full of beautiful rhymes.

~

Through ups and downs, keep pushing through,
You have the strength to make dreams come true.
No matter what challenges lie ahead,
Have faith in yourself, for success is widespread.

~

But you know what you are achieving,
No need for rhyming or deceiving,
You're focused on your goals, never retreating.

~

Going to college and gaining knowledge,
Building a career that will never falter,
Your determination will make you the victor.

~

With every step forward, your confidence is increasing,
Negativity and doubt, you are releasing.
Rest assured, success is within your reaching.

The Wrong Pearls

Time: 1:47 am
Date: 20.2.15

There was a time when my life was filled with rhyme,
Every day was like a sweet little chime.
I didn't have a care, just me and my flair,
Dancing through the world without a single tear.

~

But then I met Mark, who left me in the dark, his words
were Sharp like an arrow hitting its mark.
He took away my joy, like a thief in the night,
Leaving me alone to face the fight.

~

I picked up the pieces, found strength within myself,
Determined to put him on the shelf.
With each passing day, I grew stronger in my own way,
No longer willing to be someone's prey.

~

I embraced my independence, with confidence and pride,
No longer willing to let anyone decide.
I built a life of my own, where happiness had grown,
Leaving behind the pain that once was known.

~

So here I stand today, with a heart that's free to play,
No longer bound by sorrow or dismay.
Life may have thrown its curveballs my way,
But I've learned to rise above and live each day.

Giving Up

Time: 22:18pm
Date: 3.12.14

Listen, I understand that at times you may feel disheartened
And lacking inspiration,
But that should never hinder you from pursuing your
deepest aspirations.

~

Who said you had to call it quits and retire?
Let your determination burn bright like a raging fire.

~

I know exhaustion may have set in and you might be tired,
But don't lose hope, keep pushing forward, your dream
could still be acquired!

~

Your potential has not yet expired,
So go out there and fulfill what is required,
Dream big, aim higher and see your desires transpire.

~

Dream of those luxurious houses and sleek cars that you
have Always admired,
Now is the time to set your sights even higher,
Never let your ambition be mired.

~

Stay motivated every step of the way,
Empower yourself to seize each new day,
And don't resort to cowardice by running away.

Released

Time: 2:24am
Date: 19.2.2015

From the north, south, west, and east,
I see the sun shining, and my blessings are released.
As I walk in this world, my spirit is at peace.
The rhythm of life flows through me like a gentle breeze.
I find solace in nature's rhyme, where every creature has its own time.

~

In the morning's embrace, I feel the warmth on my face.
The beauty of the day unfolds with grace.
With each step I take, I leave behind any trace of worry or fear that once held me in place.

~

I am a melody, harmonizing with the universe's symphony.
In this vast cosmic tapestry, I find my purpose and identity.
Like a river that flows to the sea, my soul is free and wild and forever will be.

~

With gratitude in my heart and love as my guide,
Abundance finds its way to me from every side.
Opportunities align and success becomes my stride.
In this dance of life, there's no need to hide.

~

So let me bask in the sunlight's golden glow.
Let me embrace each moment as it comes and goes.

For in this journey called life, I've come to know that when
we align with our truth, our blessings overflow.

~

From the north, south, west, and east,
I see the sun shining bright at its peak.
My heart sings with joy as my blessings continue to speak.
With each passing day, my spirit feels complete.

~

I am released from all that once weighed me down.
In this newfound freedom, true happiness is found.
As I journey through life's ups and downs,
I know that miracles abound.

~

So let us embrace the rhyme of existence and dance to its
Eternal cadence.
Let us celebrate each moment with gratitude and reverence.
For in this grand tapestry of life's magnificence,
We find our true essence.

~

From sunrise to sunset, let us shine our light so bright.
Let us spread love and kindness with all our might.
For in the end, it's the love we give and receive that ignites
our inner light.

~

I am a vessel of love and peace,
Connected to all that is, from west to east.
My soul finds solace in nature's rhyme,
Where every beat brings forth divine.
And as I walk this earthly path,
I know that blessings will forever last.

Pins And Needles

Time: 4:02am
Date: 19.2.15

There are people who will hurt you, with pins and needles,
Some are so blind they have demons in their vehicles,
They are lethal,
Acting like they are a part of society and they are equal,
But deep down in their hearts, they know that they are very deceitful.

~

Out there acting peaceful,
Helping people with their cars, by adding diesel,
But God truly knows that every bone in them is evil.
Acting feeble, reading their bibles and attending the right cathedral, but still having the attitude of an old, medieval.

~

In this world of rhyme and reason,
Their actions may change with each passing season.
But their true nature remains constant, like a hidden treason. Beware of those who mask themselves with false appeasement. For behind their smiles lies a darkness that cannot be seized. They may offer assistance to those in need, Yet beneath the surface, their ulterior motives breed.

Who's Wrong?

Time: 11:58pm
Date: 19.2.15

Stupid arguments,
They never really last very long.
Me and my husband, both know that this is wrong.

~

His words may flow like a silly rhyme,
But deep down, he's just wasting time.
I can see through his weak facade,
And I won't be fooled by his act so flawed.

~

Blah, blah, blah! He keeps singing along,
But I'll stay strong and prove him wrong.
I'll show him that strength isn't just about might,
It's about listening and finding common ground in this fight.

~

So, I kissed him on the lips and said with a grin,
"Let's put an end to this silly din."
But he stubbornly replied,
"No, you're mistaken,
I am a man, and I won't be shaken."

~

I sighed and thought, if he doesn't change his song,
I might just have to board that plane to Hong Kong.

Reconsider

Time: 1:31am
Date: 20.2.15

She said listen, "When I was 15, I was a pretty little stripper,
I was working 9-5 and I didn't have a tipper."

~

"I was a school-skipper, Cause my mama was just always on a dicker, What was I supposed to do?
Yes, I grew up a little quicker."

~

But I'm no quitter.
There was a point, when I had my fingers on the trigger,
I was smoking every night, drinking up my malt liquor.
Please reconsider, I will never be a little gold digger.

~

I'm a big woman now,
I grew up to be a winner;
Ask the vicar.
Life threw me curveballs, but I became a rhyme scribe.
From humble beginnings as an underdog with nothing to hide, I let my words flow like a smooth-talking guide.

~

With each verse, my voice gets amplified,
My rhymes break barriers and reach far and wide.
No longer defined by the past or anyone's deride.

~

I've learned to rise above the tide,
Turning obstacles into stepping stones with pride.
With every line, my spirit can't be denied.

The Mourner

Time: 3:01
Date: 20.2.15

I don't want to dwell in sorrow,
Mourning over a coffin's shadow.
Instead, I aspire to be a beacon of positivity,
An informer who's admired and adored.

~

I long to be a catalyst for transformation,
With properties along the shore.
A helping hand to farmers,
ensuring their cornfields thrive in galore,

~

All while putting in hard work and giving it my all,
Never feeling sore.
No more endless mourning,
No more lamenting at dawn,
I've ceased my yawning,
Now ready for a new dawn.

~

I can't bear this mundane existence any longer,
I crave something more,
The sun's rays seem distant as if they've forgotten to perform, Though I miss you dearly, this monotonous routine has Become a bore.

The Better You Get

Time: 15:56
Date: 14/07/24

And then you realize,
That the longer you do something,
The better you get at it,
Train hard, and watch your skills grow bit by bit.

~

With every repetition and every stride,
You'll discover new strengths you'll never want to hide.
Push through the challenges, embrace the sweat,
For with dedication and perseverance, success you'll get.

~

So don't shy away from the effort it takes,
For greatness awaits those who refuse to break.

Until it's my time, I will write.

**With love,
Chavanese Wint**

www.ingramcontent.com/pod-product-compliance
Lightning Source LLC
Chambersburg PA
CBHW070438010526
44118CB00014B/2102